world of
ERiC CARLE™
PRESCHOOL
WORKBOOK

Help your child learn essential school readiness skills with
the World of Eric Carle! With over 100 pages of activities,
this workbook was developed by educational experts and aligns
with national pre-kindergarten early learning standards.

written by Wiley Blevins

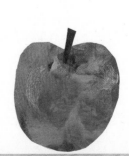

WORLD OF ERIC CARLE
An imprint of Penguin Random House LLC, New York

First published in the United States of America by World of Eric Carle,
an imprint of Penguin Random House LLC, New York, 2021

Copyright © 2021 by Penguin Random House LLC

To find out more about Eric Carle and his books, please visit eric-carle.com.
To learn about The Eric Carle Museum of Picture Book Art, please visit carlemuseum.org.

Visit us online at penguinrandomhouse.com.

Printed in the United States of America

ISBN 9780593386200   10 9 8 7 6 5 4   COMM

Designed by Dinardo Design

The World of Eric Carle nurtures a child's love of literature and learning, encouraging imaginative play and exploration. Trusted by parents, teachers, and librarians, and beloved by children worldwide for generations, *The Very Hungry Caterpillar* and other timeless storybooks come to life in colorfully creative products designed to inspire very hungry young minds.

The **WORLD OF ERIC CARLE Preschool Workbook** covers these and other important early learning concepts:

- the ABCs
- letters and sounds
- pre-writing strokes
- numbers
- counting
- patterns
- colors
- shapes

Follow these steps to get the most benefit from the workbook:

- Find a time when your child is ready to engage in the activities.
- Keep the learning sessions brief.
- Engage your child in talk about the target skill on each page. Remember: You are your child's first and most important teacher.
- Be positive and encouraging.
- Foster creativity and look for ways to connect skills to other activities throughout the day. For example, help your child count objects when you gather items for cooking or put away toys. Look for objects at home whose names begin with a specific sound. Have your child practice tracing, writing, and building with letter cards of their name.

Draw to Write

Can you help the animal find its food?

 Trace each line.

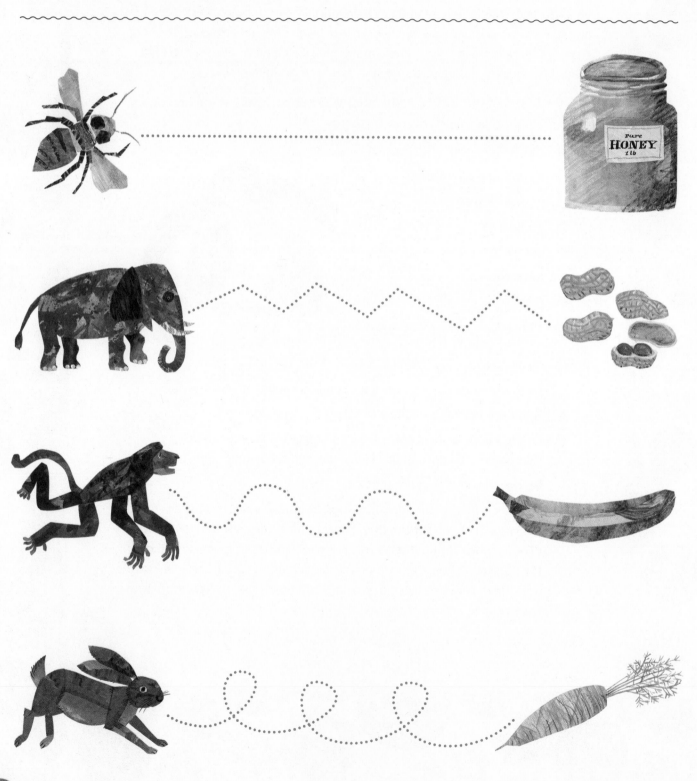

Can you help everyone find their home?

Trace each line.

Draw to Write

 Trace the circles and lines to make a sun.

1

2

3

4

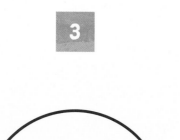

Draw and color a sun.

Trace the shapes and lines to make a house.

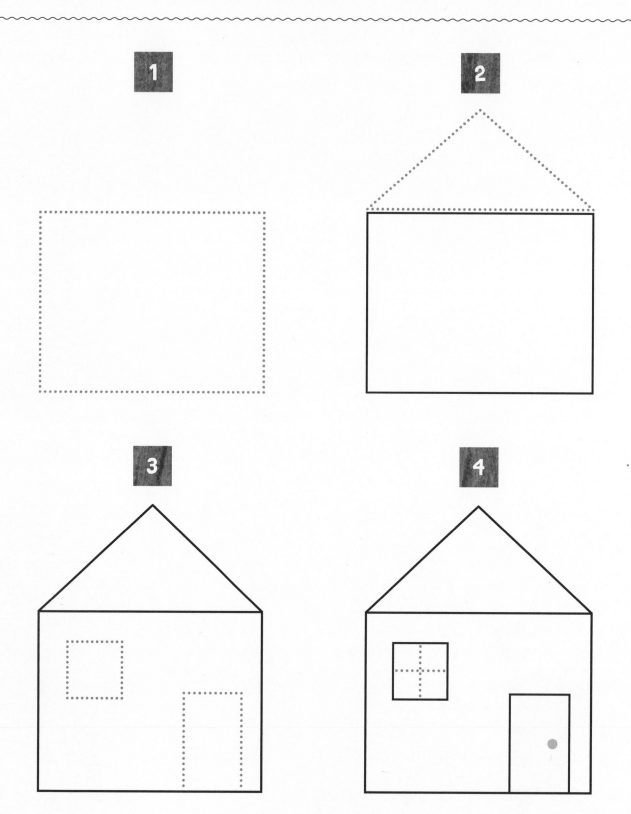

Draw and color a house.

The apple is red.

Can you color each apple red?

The frog is green.

Can you color each frog green?

The bird is blue.

 Can you ⟨circle⟩ each blue picture?

A chick is yellow.

 **Can you color each yellow item?**

The bear is brown.

 Can you (circle) each brown picture?

A zebra is black and white.

Can you (circle) each animal that is black and white?

An orange is orange.

Can you color each orange item?

The flower is pink.

 Can you color each cupcake pink?

The grapes are purple.

 Can you (circle) each purple picture?

A rainbow has many colors.

Color the rainbow.

Can you name each color you use?

A circle is round like a ball.

✏️ **Color the BIG circles red.**

✏️ **Color the little circles blue.**

Can you trace the circle?

Color each circle red.

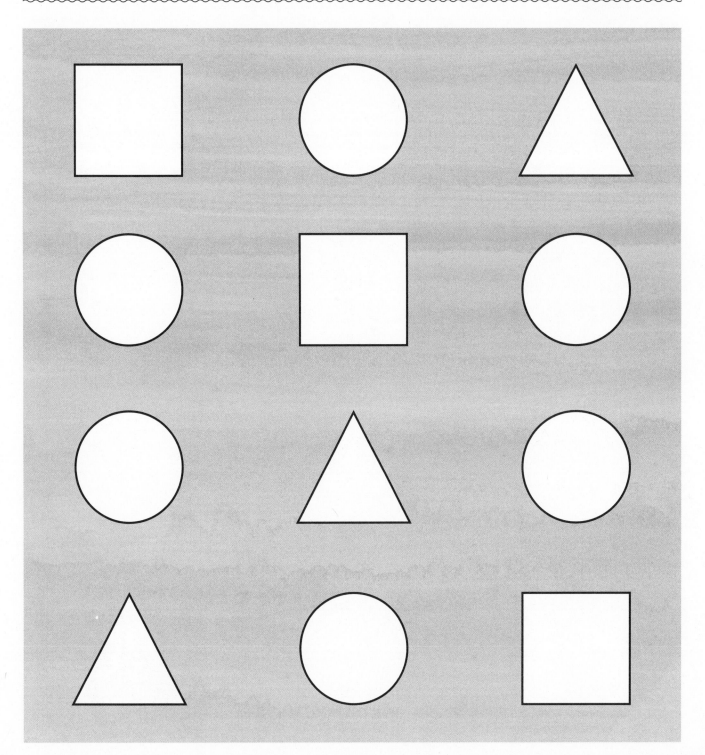

Shapes

A square has 4 sides.

Each side is the same size.

Help the butterfly find the flowers.

 **Connect the squares to make a path.**

Start

    End

Can you trace the square?
Color each square orange.

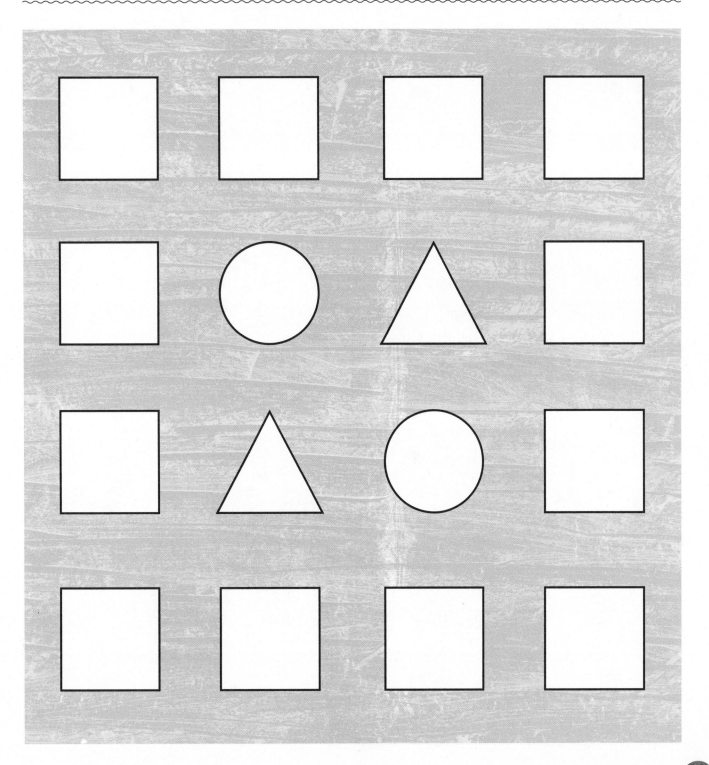

A triangle has 3 sides.

 **Color the triangles in the picture.**

Can you trace the triangle?

Color each triangle green.

A rectangle has 4 sides.

2 sides are long. 2 sides are short.

Help the cow get to the barn.

Connect the rectangles to make a path.

Start

End

Can you trace the rectangle?

Color each rectangle purple.

These are the uppercase, or capital, letters.

Can you say each letter name?

Circle the first letter in your name.

A B C D
E F G H I J K
L M N O P
Q R S T U V
W X Y Z

These are the lowercase, or small, letters.

Can you say each letter name?

Write your name in the box using uppercase for the first letter and lowercase for the rest.

a b c d
e f g h i j k
l m n o p
q r s t u v
w x y z

Can you trace the letter *Aa*?

alligator

~~~~~~

What is it?

 Color each capital A and small *a* red to find out.

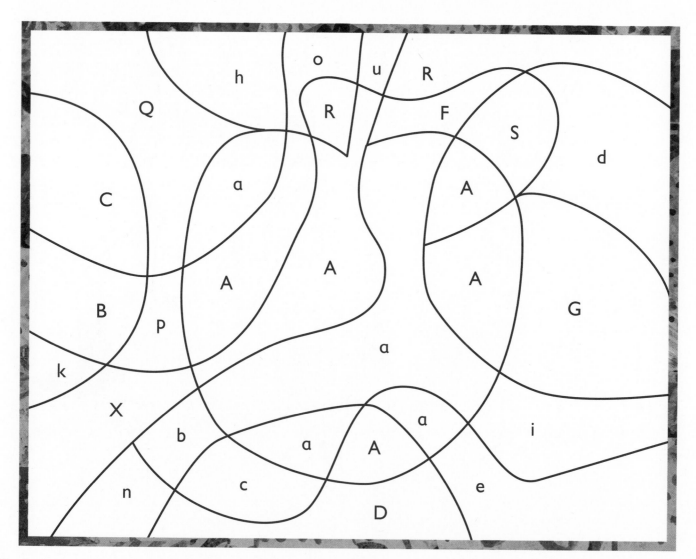

Can you trace the letter *Bb*?

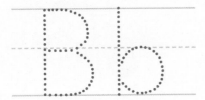

butterfly

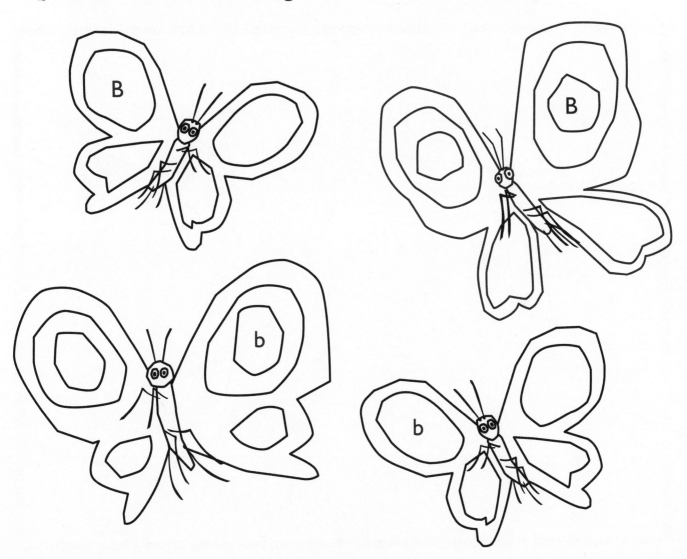

Color each butterfly with a capital *B* blue.

Color each butterfly with a small *b* orange.

Can you trace the letter *Cc*?

car

What is it?

Color each capital **C** and small **c** orange to find out.

Can you trace the letter *Dd*?

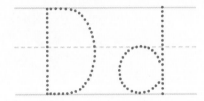

dog

Color each dog with a capital *D* or small *d* on it.

Can you trace the letter *Ee*?

egg

 Color each egg with a capital **E** or small **e** on it.

Can you trace the letter *Ff*?

flower

~~~~~~

 Color each flower with a capital *F* or small *f* on it.

Can you trace the letter *Gg*?

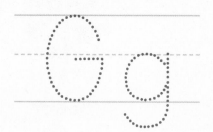

grapes

What is it?

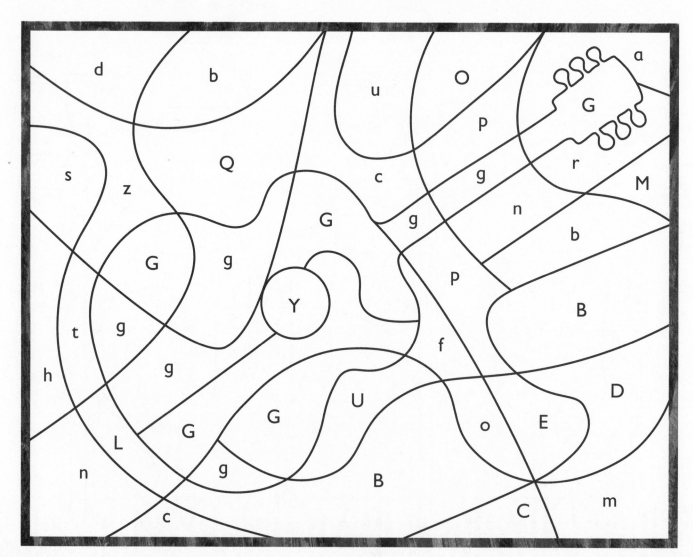

Color each capital **G** and small *g* brown to find out.

Can you trace the letter *Hh*?

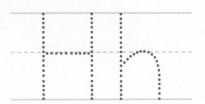

heart

Connect the dots in order from *A* to *H*.

What did you make?

Can you trace the letter *Ii*?

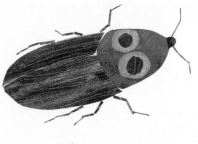

insect

 Color each insect with a capital *I* or small *i* on it.

Can you trace the letter *Jj*?

jelly beans

✏️ Color each jelly bean with a capital *J* or small *j* on it.

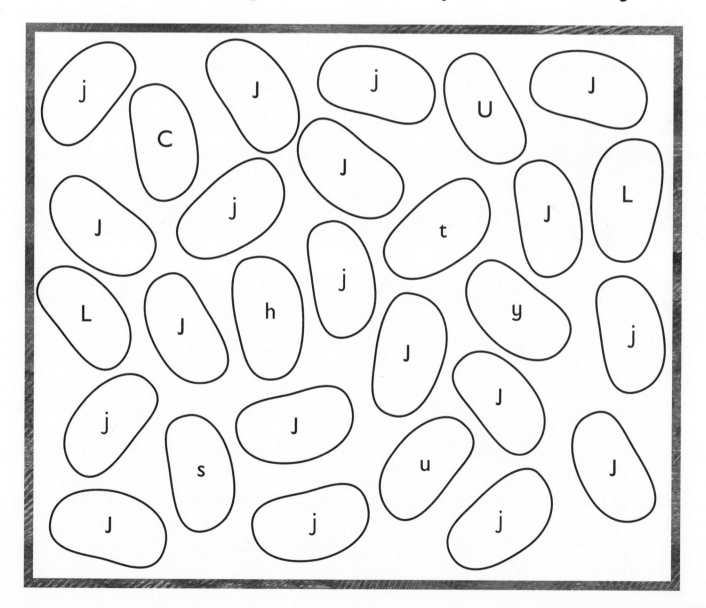

Can you trace the letter _Kk_?

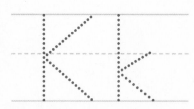

kangaroo

What is it?

Color each capital _K_ and small _k_ purple to find out.

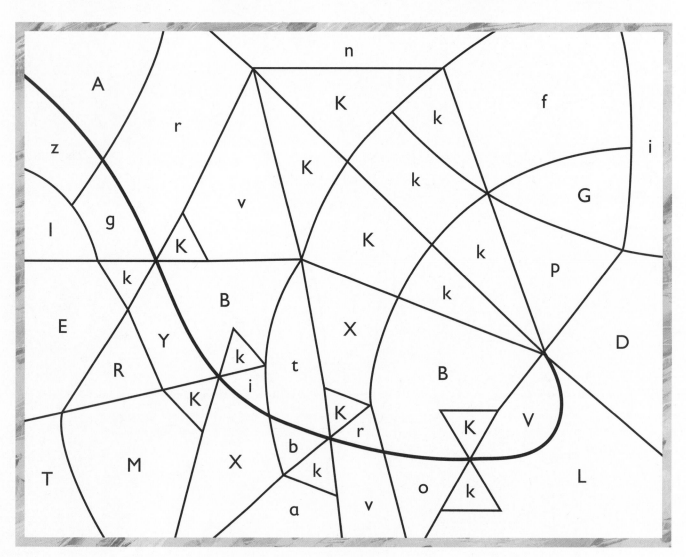

Can you trace the letter *Ll*?

leaf

 Color each leaf with a capital *L* or small *l* on it.

Can you trace the letter Mm?

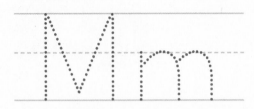

monkey

What is it?

Color each capital **M** and small **m** black to find out.

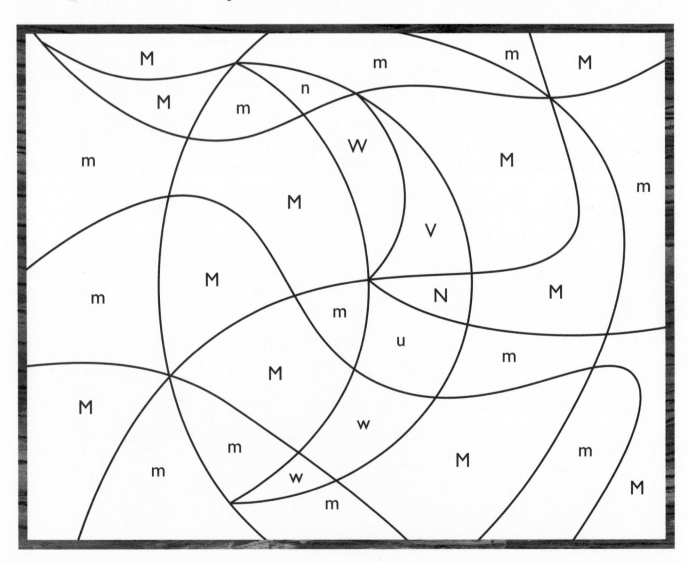

Can you trace the letter *Nn*?

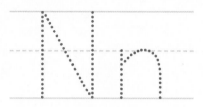

nest

 Color each number blue.

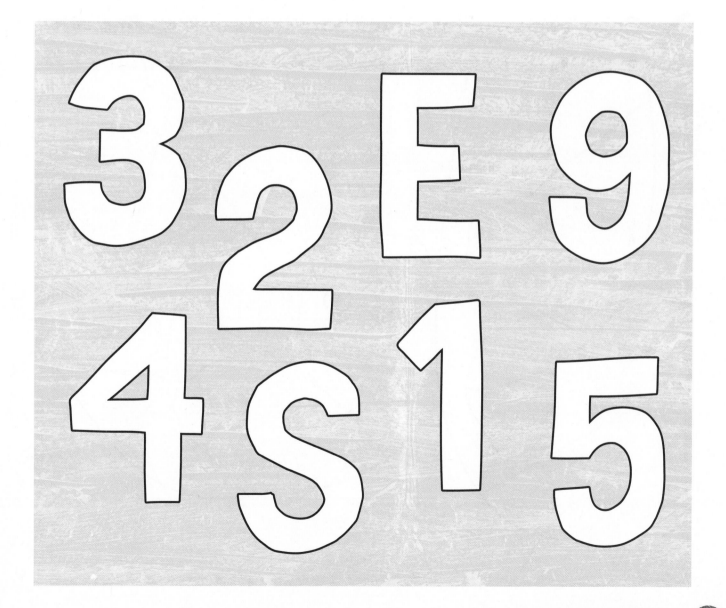

Can you trace the letter Oo?

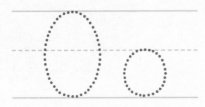

octopus

What is it?

Color each capital O and small o brown to find out.

Can you trace the letter *Pp*?

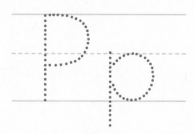

pumpkin

Connect the dots in order from *A* to *P*.

What did you make?

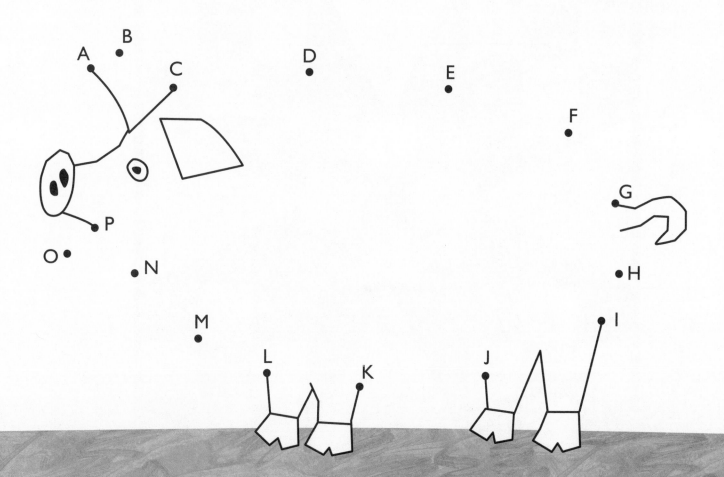

Can you trace the letter Qq?

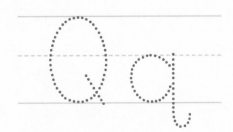

quilt

✎ **Color each capital Q and small q yellow to finish the quilt.**

Can you trace the letter *Rr*?

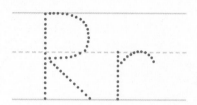

rooster

What is it?

Color each capital *R* and small *r* red to find out.

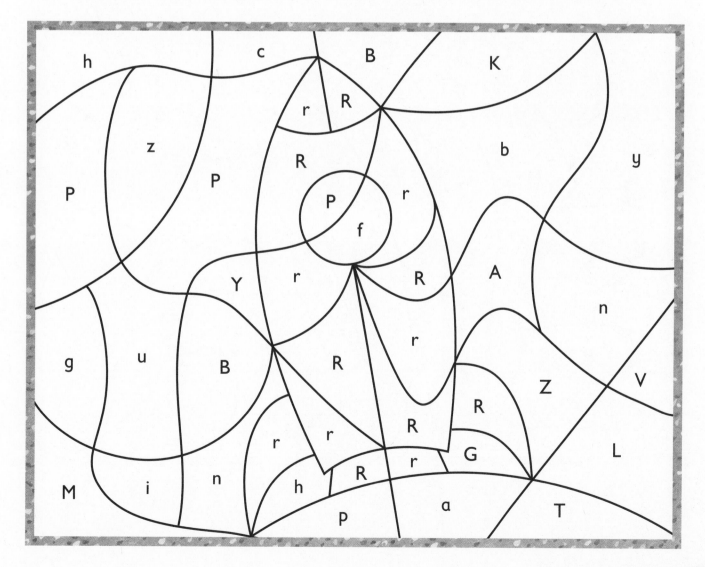

Can you trace the letter Ss?

sun

What is it?

Color each capital S and small s green to find out.

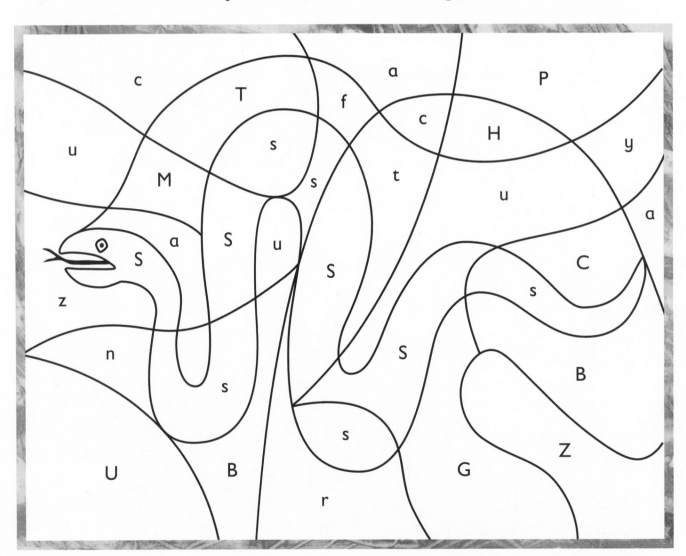

Can you trace the letter *Tt*?

truck

Connect the dots in order from *A* to *T*.

What did you make?

Can you trace the letter _Uu_?

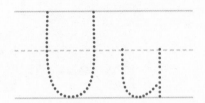

umbrella

🖍 **Color each umbrella with a capital _U_ or small _u_ on it.**

Can you trace the letter Vv?

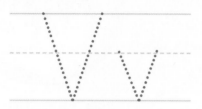

volcano

What is it?

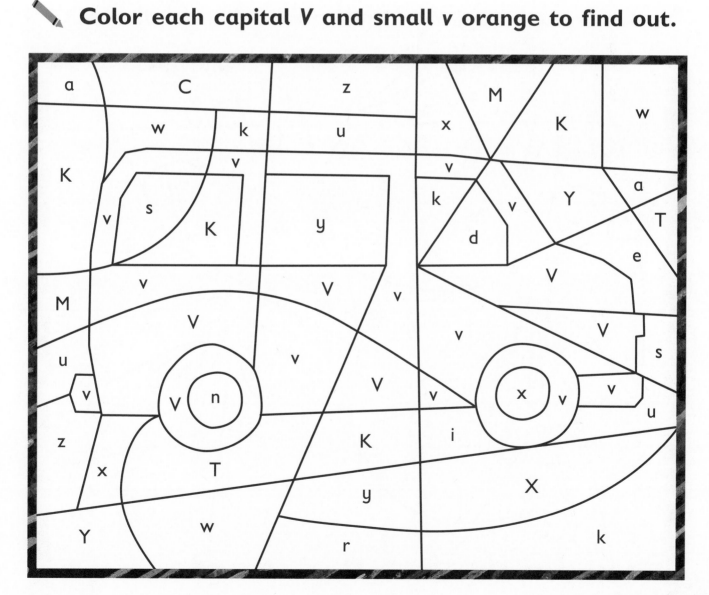

Color each capital **V** and small **v** orange to find out.

Can you trace the letter Ww?

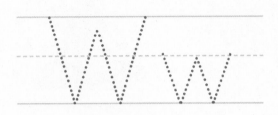

watermelon

What is it?

Color each capital W and small w blue to find out.

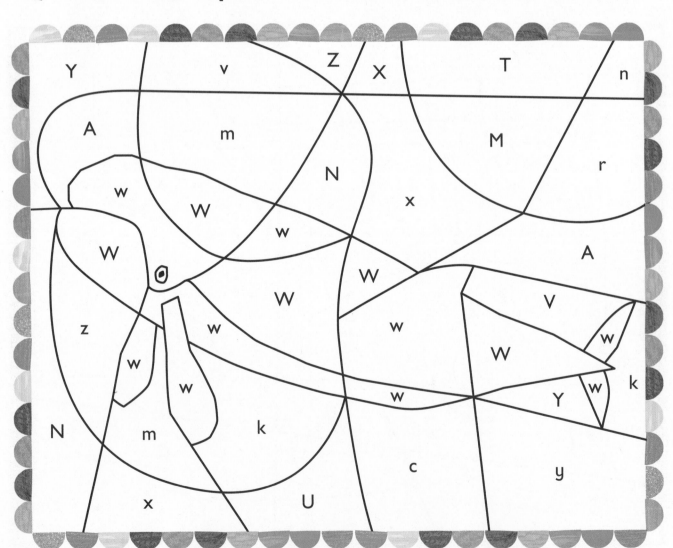

Can you trace the letter Xx?

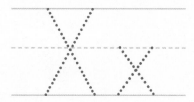

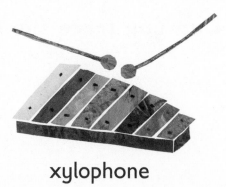

xylophone

Color each part of the xylophone with a capital **X** or small **x** on it.

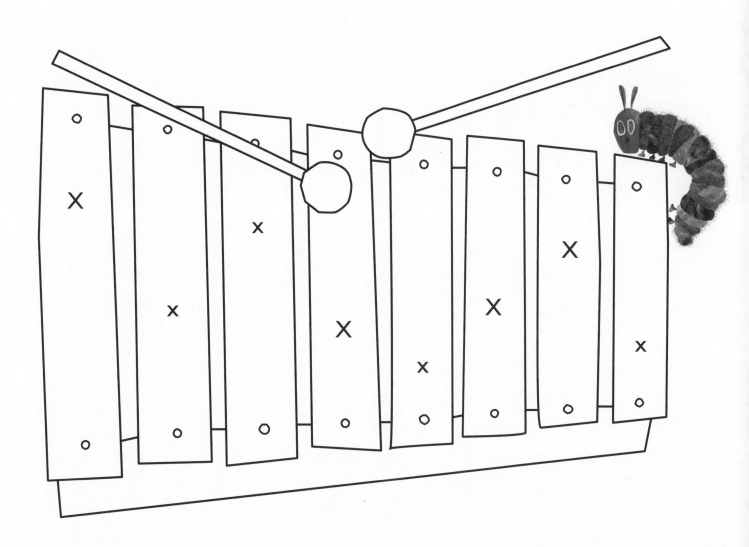

Can you trace the letter Yy?

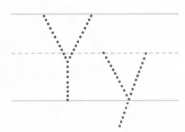

yo-yo

 Color each yo-yo with a capital Y or small y on it.

Can you trace the letter Zz?

zipper

 Connect the dots in order from A to Z.

What did you make?

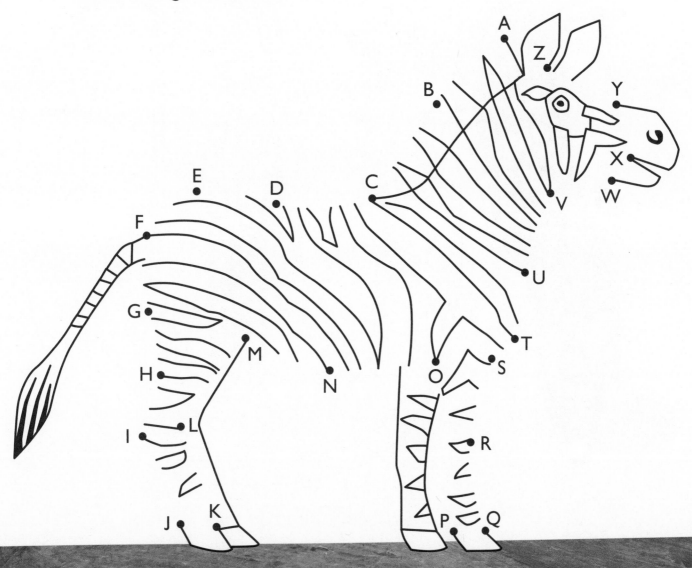

The Very Hungry Caterpillar ate 1 apple.

Can you color 1 apple red?

The child needs 2 shoes.

Can you color the 2 shoes blue?

Numbers

The cake has 3 hearts on it.

 Can you color the 3 hearts pink?

The bear eats 4 jars of honey.

 Can you color the 4 jars orange?

The cake has 5 candles on it.

 Can you color the 5 candles purple?

Santa brings 6 gifts.

Can you color the 6 gifts green?

The child picks 7 pretty flowers.

 Can you color the 7 flowers red?

The child kicks 8 balls.

✎ **Can you color the 8 balls black?**

9 birds are flying from the trees.

 Can you color the 9 birds brown?

10 little rubber ducks float out at sea.

Can you color the 10 ducks yellow?

Can you count to 3?

1 **2** **3**

● ●● ●●●

〰〰〰〰〰〰〰〰〰〰〰〰〰〰〰〰〰〰〰〰〰

Read the number.

Color that number of objects.

Can you trace the numbers?

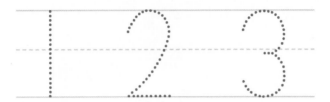

Count the number of objects in each row.
Write the number on the line.

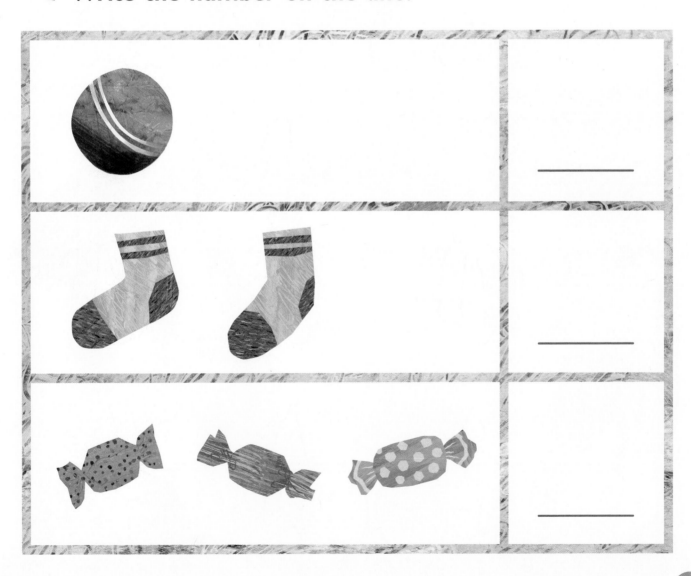

Can you count to 5?

1 2 3 4 5

Color 5 balls.

Can you trace the numbers?

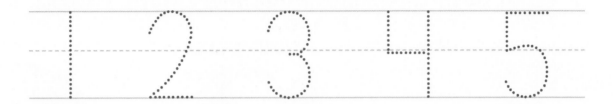

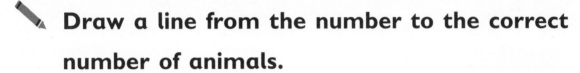

✏️ **Draw a line from the number to the correct number of animals.**

Help The Very Hungry Caterpillar turn into a butterfly.
Trace a path through the numbers from 1 to 10.

Connect the dots from 1 to 10.

What animal home did you make?

Count the number of objects in each row.

Write the number on the line.

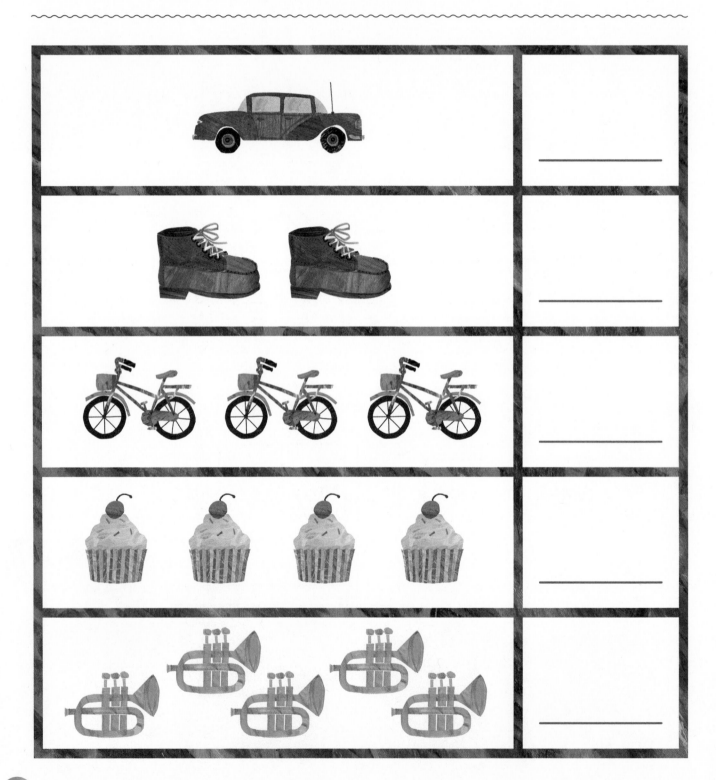

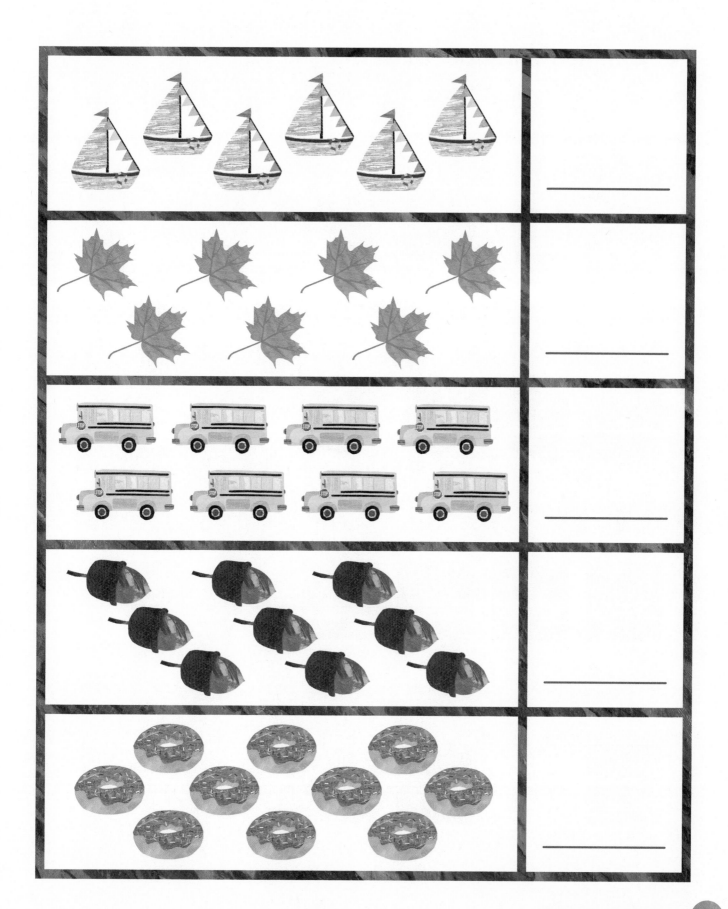

Can you finish the pattern?

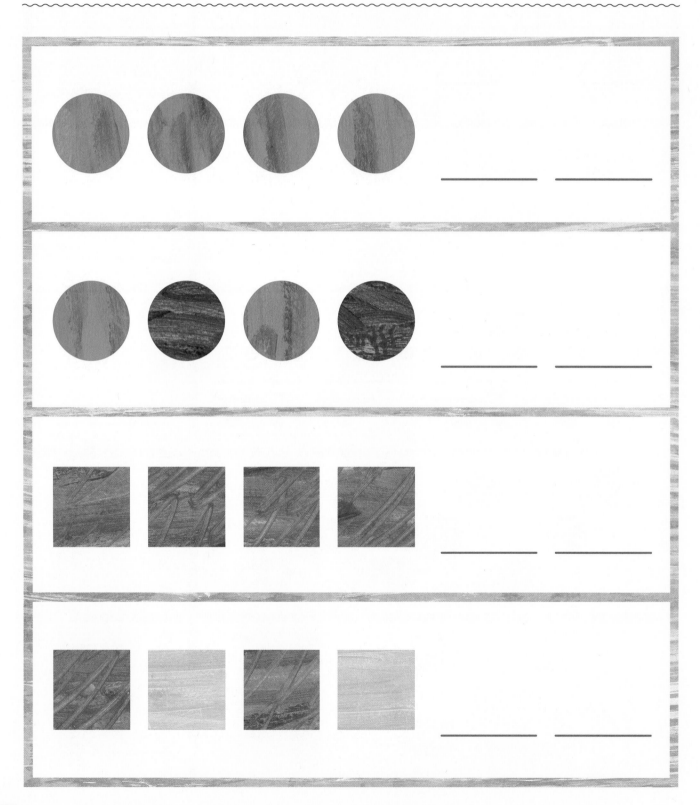

Can you finish the pattern?

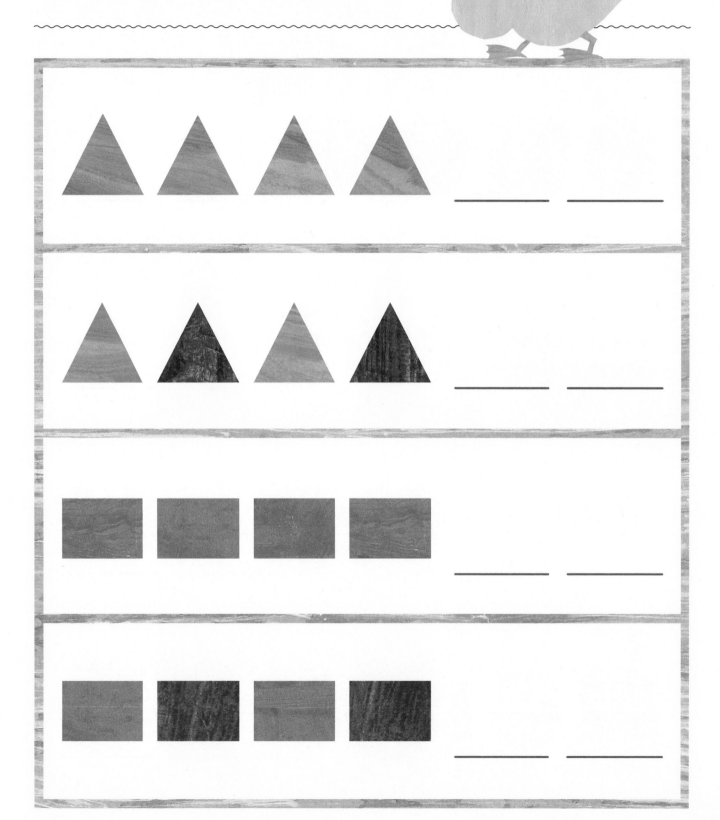

Patterns

 Can you finish the pattern?

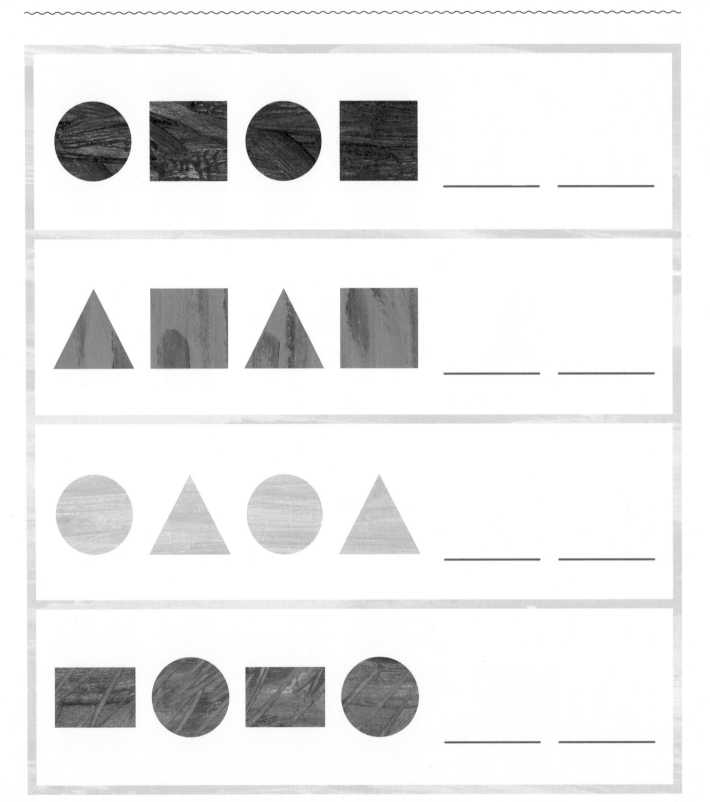

Can you finish the pattern?

Can you finish the pattern?

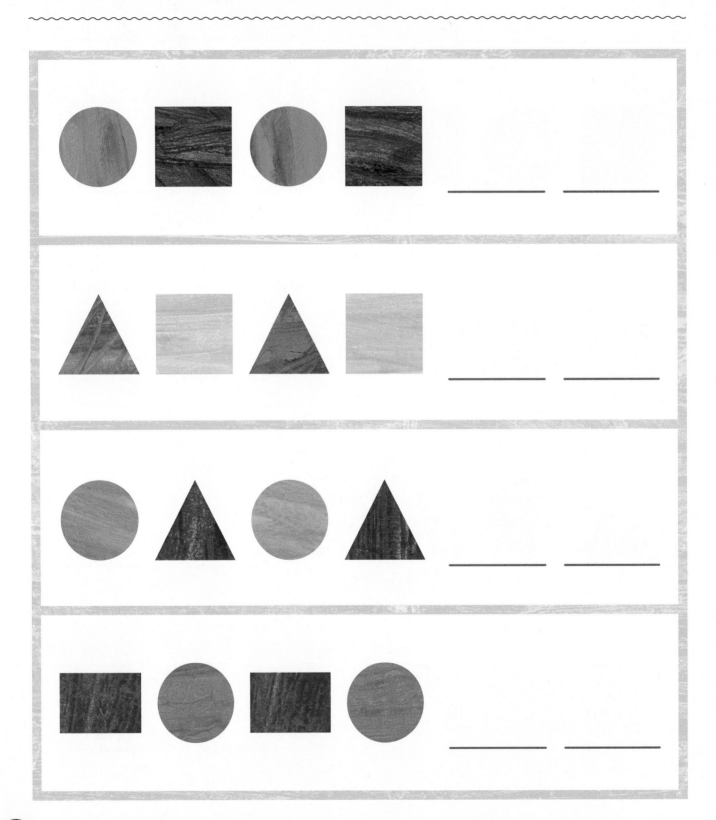

Can you finish the pattern?

Aa as in acorn or apple

✏️ **Color each acorn brown.**

✏️ **Color each apple red.**

✏️ **Trace and write Aa.**

Say the sounds for Aa when you write the letter.

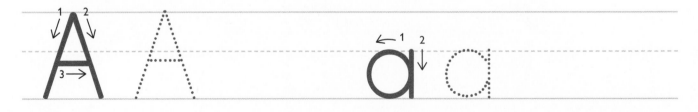

Bb as in bear

✏️ **Color each picture that begins with *Bb*.**

✏️ **Trace and write *Bb*.**

Say the sound for *Bb* when you write the letter.

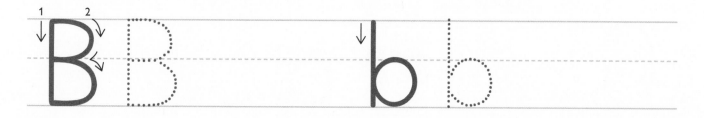

Cc as in cow

Can you help The Very Hungry Caterpillar find the cupcake?

Trace the path of cupcakes through the maze.

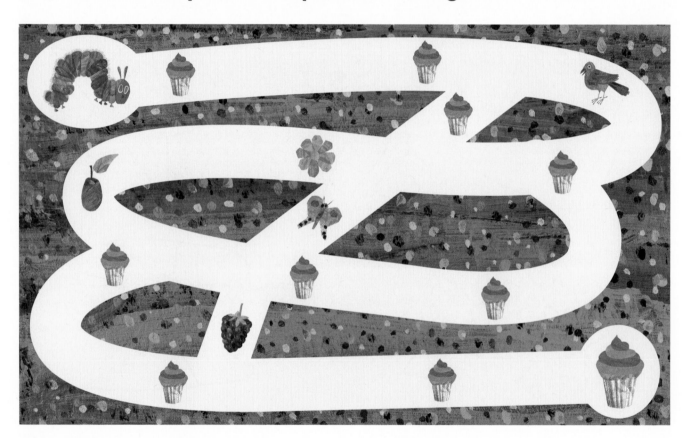

Trace and write Cc.

Say the sound for Cc when you write the letter.

Dd as in dinosaur

✏️ (Circle) each picture that begins with *Dd*.

✏️ **Trace and write *Dd*.**

Say the sound for *Dd* when you write the letter.

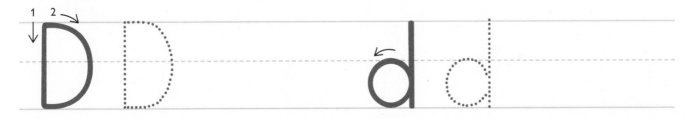

Ee as in eagle or elephant

✏️ **Color each eagle brown.**

✏️ **Color each elephant gray.**

✏️ **Trace and write *Ee*.**

Say the sounds for *Ee* when you write the letter.

Ff as in fish

✏️ **Color each picture that begins with *Ff*.**

✏️ **Trace and write *Ff*.**

Say the sound for *Ff* when you write the letter.

Gg as in grapes

Can you help the goat find the grass?

✏️ **Trace the path of goats through the maze.**

✏️ **Trace and write Gg.**

Say the sound for Gg when you write the letter.

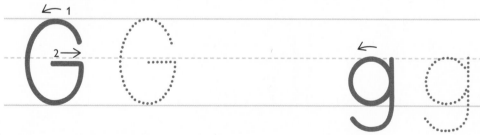

Hh as in horse

✏️ **Color each picture that begins with Hh.**

✏️ **Trace and write Hh.**

Say the sound for Hh when you write the letter.

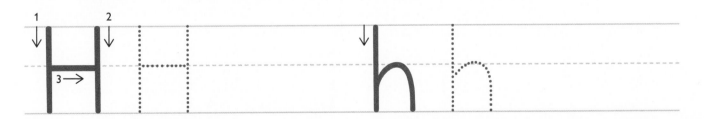

Ii as in ice cream or insect

Can you help the kids find the ice cream truck?

Trace the path of ice cream cones through the maze.

Trace and write _Ii_.

Say the sounds for _Ii_ when you write the letter.

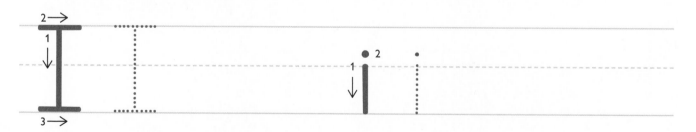

Jj  as in jam

✏️ **Color each jar purple.**

✏️ **Color each jacket red.**

✏️ **Trace and write *Jj*.**

Say the sound for *Jj* when you write the letter.

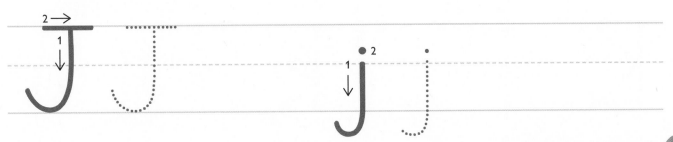

Kk as in key

Circle each picture that begins with *Kk*.

Trace and write *Kk*.

Say the sound for *Kk* when you write the letter.

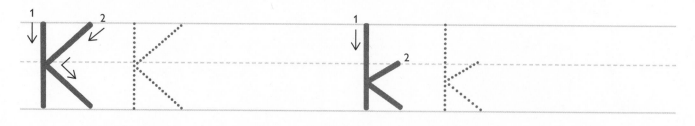

Ll as in lion

Circle each picture that begins with *Ll*.

Trace and write *Ll*.

Say the sound for *Ll* when you write the letter.

Mm as in mouse

✏ (Circle) each picture that begins with **Mm**.

✏ **Trace and write Mm.**

Say the sound for Mm when you write the letter.

Nn as in noodles

Can you help the bird get to the nest?

Trace the path of nests through the maze.

Trace and write *Nn*.

Say the sound for *Nn* when you write the letter.

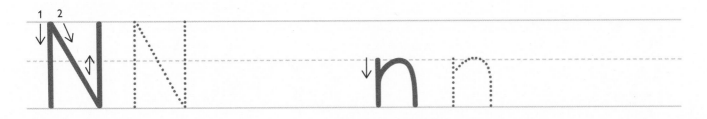

Oo as in ocean or octopus

Color the ocean blue.

Color each octopus pink.

Trace and write Oo.

Say the sounds for Oo when you write the letter.

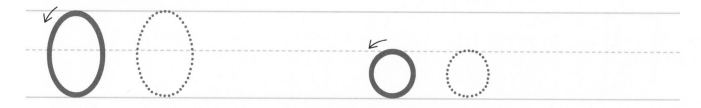

Pp as in pineapple

✏️ **Color each picture that begins with *Pp*.**

✏️ **Trace and write *Pp*.**

Say the sound for *Pp* when you write the letter.

Qq as in queen

Can you help the queen get to the king?

 Trace the queen's path through the maze.

Trace and write *Qq*.

Say the sound for **Qq** when you write the letter.

Q Q   q q

Rr as in rainbow

✏️ (Circle) each picture that begins with *Rr*.

✏️ **Trace and write *Rr*.**

Say the sound for *Rr* when you write the letter.

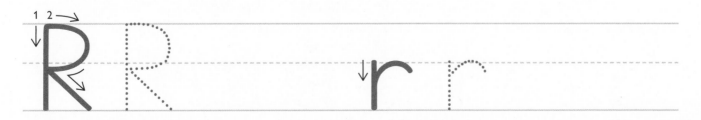

Ss as in spider

✏️ **Color each picture that begins with Ss.**

✏️ **Trace and write Ss.**

Say the sound for Ss when you write the letter.

S S   S s

Tt as in trumpet

✏️ (Circle) each picture that begins with *Tt*.

✏️ **Trace and write *Tt*.**

Say the sound for *Tt* when you write the letter.

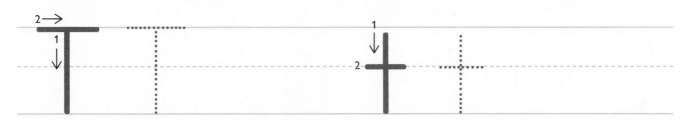

Uu as in unicorn or umbrella

✏️ **Color each unicorn pink.**

✏️ **Color each umbrella purple.**

✏️ **Trace and write *Uu*.**

Say the sounds for *Uu* when you write the letter.

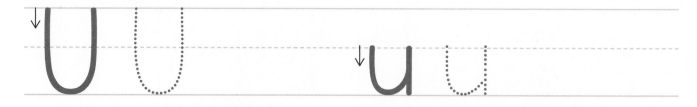

V v as in violin

Can you put the flowers in the vase?

Trace the path of flowers through the maze.

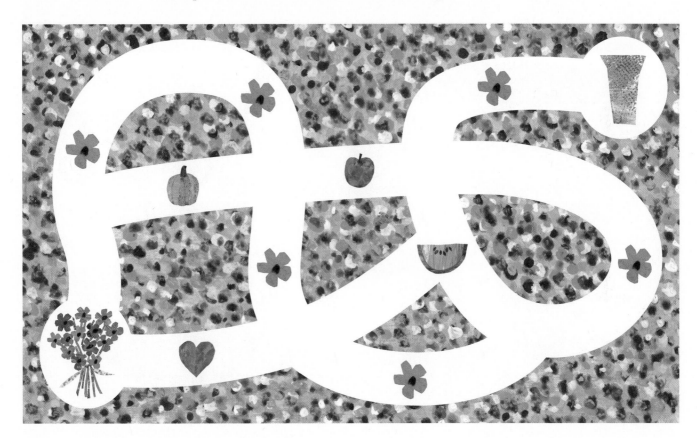

Trace and write *Vv*.

Say the sound for *Vv* when you write the letter.

Ww as in walrus

✏️ (Circle) each picture that begins with *Ww*.

✏️ **Trace and write *Ww*.**

Say the sound for *Ww* when you write the letter.

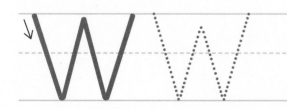 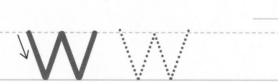

Xx  as in X-ray

Can you help the child find the fox?

✏️ **Trace the path of foxes through the maze.**

✏️ **Trace and write Xx.**

Say the sound for Xx when you write the letter.

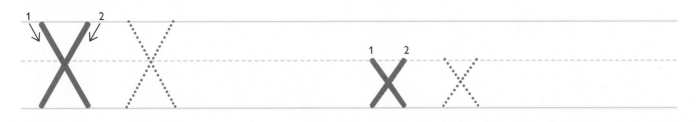

Yy as in yellow yo-yo

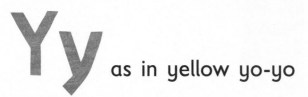

✏️ (Circle) each object that is yellow, like the yellow yo-yo.

✏️ **Trace and write Yy.**

Say the sound for Yy when you write the letter.

Zz as in zebra

Can you help the zebra find the zoo?

✏️ **Trace the path of zebras through the maze.**

✏️ **Trace and write Zz.**

Say the sound for Zz when you write the letter.

Z Z   z z

Answer Key

Draw to Write

Can you help the animal find its food?
✎ Trace each line.

4

Draw to Write

Can you help everyone find their home?
✎ Trace each line.

5

Draw to Write

✎ Trace the circles and lines to make a sun.

6

✎ Draw and color a sun.

Drawings will vary.

7

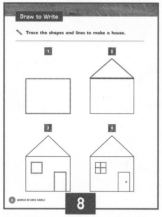

Draw to Write

✎ Trace the shapes and lines to make a house.

8

✎ Draw and color a house.

Drawings will vary.

9

Colors

The apple is red.
✎ Can you color each apple red?

10

The frog is green.
✎ Can you color each frog green?

11

Colors

The bird is blue.
✎ Can you (circle) each blue picture?

12

A chick is yellow.
✎ Can you color each yellow item?

13

Colors

The bear is brown.
✎ Can you (circle) each brown picture?

14

A zebra is black and white.
✎ Can you (circle) each animal that is black and white?

15

Colors

An orange is orange.
✎ Can you color each orange item?

16

The flower is pink.
✎ Can you color each cupcake pink?

17

Colors

The grapes are purple.
✎ Can you (circle) each purple picture?

18

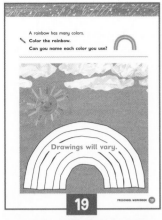

A rainbow has many colors.
Color the rainbow.
Can you name each color you use?

Drawings will vary.

19

Shapes

A circle is round like a ball.
Color the BIG circles red.
Color the little circles blue.

Red   Red
Red Blue
Blue Blue

20 WORLD OF ERIC CARLE

Can you trace the circle?
Color each circle red.

21 PRESCHOOL WORKBOOK

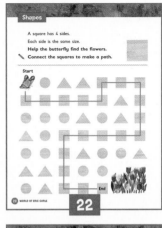

Shapes

A square has 4 sides.
Each side is the same size.
Help the butterfly find the flowers.
Connect the squares to make a path.

Start

End

22 WORLD OF ERIC CARLE

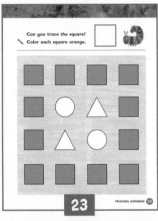

Can you trace the square?
Color each square orange.

23 PRESCHOOL WORKBOOK

Shapes

A triangle has 3 sides.
Color the triangles in the picture.

24 WORLD OF ERIC CARLE

Can you trace the triangle?
Color each triangle green.

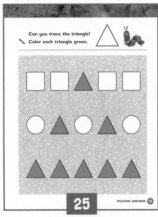

25 PRESCHOOL WORKBOOK

Shapes

A rectangle has 4 sides.
2 sides are long. 2 sides are short.
Help the cow get to the barn.
Connect the rectangles to make a path.

Start

End

26 WORLD OF ERIC CARLE

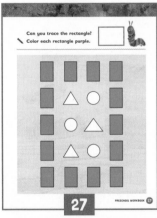

Can you trace the rectangle?
Color each rectangle purple.

27 PRESCHOOL WORKBOOK

Alphabet

These are the uppercase, or capital, letters.
Can you say each letter name?
Circle the first letter in your name.

A B C D
Answers will vary.
E F G H I J K
L M N O P
Q R S T U V
W X Y Z

28 WORLD OF ERIC CARLE

These are the lowercase, or small, letters.
Can you say each letter name?
Write your name in the box using uppercase
for the first letter and lowercase for the rest.

a b c d
e f g h i j k
l m n o p
q r s t u v
w x y z

Answers will vary.

29 PRESCHOOL WORKBOOK

Alphabet

Can you trace the letter Aa?

A a
alligator

What is it?
Color each capital A and small a red to find out.

30 WORLD OF ERIC CARLE

Can you trace the letter Bb?

B b
butterfly

Color each butterfly with a capital B blue.
Color each butterfly with a small b orange.

B B
Blue Blue
b b
Orange Orange

31 PRESCHOOL WORKBOOK

Alphabet

Can you trace the letter Cc?

C c
car

What is it?
Color each capital C and small c orange to find out.

32 WORLD OF ERIC CARLE

Can you trace the letter Dd?

D d
dog

Color each dog with a capital D or small d on it.

33 PRESCHOOL WORKBOOK

Answer Key

Can you trace the letter Ee?
Ee
egg
Color each egg with a capital E or small e on it.

34

Can you trace the letter Ff?
Ff
flower
Color each flower with a capital F or small f on it.
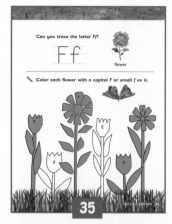
35

Alphabet
Can you trace the letter Gg?
Gg
grapes
What is it?
Color each capital G and small g brown to find out.
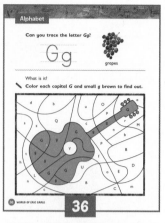
36

Can you trace the letter Hh?
Hh
heart
Connect the dots in order from A to H.
What did you make?
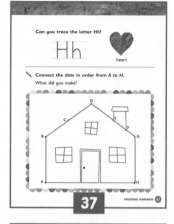
37

Alphabet
Can you trace the letter Ii?
Ii
insect
Color each insect with a capital I or small i on it.
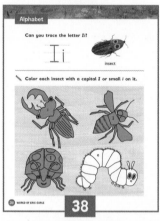
38

Can you trace the letter Jj?
Jj
jelly beans
Color each jelly bean with a capital J or small j on it.
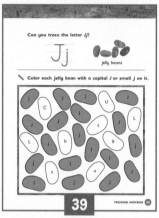
39

Alphabet
Can you trace the letter Kk?
Kk
kangaroo
What is it?
Color each capital K and small k purple to find out.
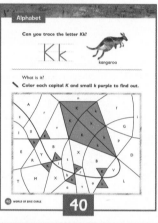
40

Can you trace the letter Ll?
Ll
leaf
Color each leaf with a capital L or small l on it.
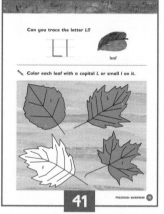
41

Alphabet
Can you trace the letter Mm?
Mm
monkey
What is it?
Color each capital M and small m black to find out.
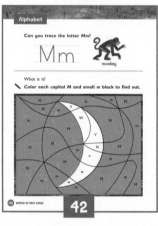
42

Can you trace the letter Nn?
Nn
nest
Color each number blue.

43

Alphabet
Can you trace the letter Oo?
Oo
octopus
What is it?
Color each capital O and small o brown to find out.
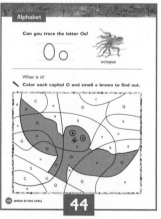
44

Can you trace the letter Pp?
Pp
pumpkin
Connect the dots in order from A to P.
What did you make?

45

Alphabet
Can you trace the letter Qq?
Qq
quilt
Color each capital Q and small q yellow to finish the quilt.
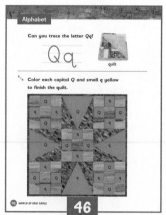
46

Can you trace the letter Rr?
Rr
rooster
What is it?
Color each capital R and small r red to find out.

47

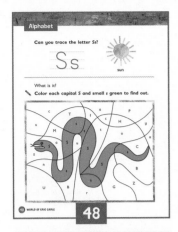

Alphabet

Can you trace the letter Ss?

S s sun

What is it?
✎ Color each capital S and small s green to find out.

48

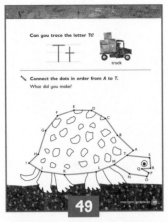

Can you trace the letter Tt?

T t truck

✎ Connect the dots in order from A to T.
What did you make?

49

Alphabet

Can you trace the letter Uu?

U u umbrella

✎ Color each umbrella with a capital U or small u on it.

50

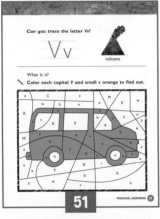

Can you trace the letter Vv?

V v volcano

What is it?
✎ Color each capital V and small v orange to find out.

51

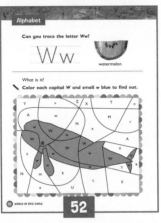

Alphabet

Can you trace the letter Ww?

W w watermelon

What is it?
✎ Color each capital W and small w blue to find out.

52

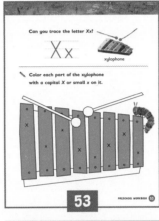

Can you trace the letter Xx?

X x xylophone

✎ Color each part of the xylophone
with a capital X or small x on it.

53

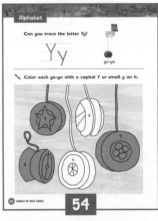

Alphabet

Can you trace the letter Yy?

Y y yo-yo

✎ Color each yo-yo with a capital Y or small y on it.

54

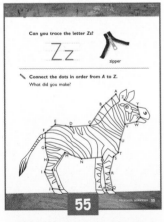

Can you trace the letter Zz?

Z z zipper

✎ Connect the dots in order from A to Z.
What did you make?

55

Numbers

The Very Hungry Caterpillar ate 1 apple.
✎ Can you color 1 apple red?

56

The child needs 2 shoes.
✎ Can you color the 2 shoes blue?

57

Numbers

The cake has 3 hearts on it.
✎ Can you color the 3 hearts pink?

58

The bear eats 4 jars of honey.
✎ Can you color the 4 jars orange?

59

Numbers

The cake has 5 candles on it.
✎ Can you color the 5 candles purple?

60

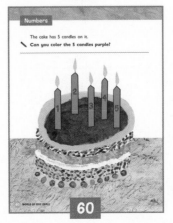

Santa brings 6 gifts.
✎ Can you color the 6 gifts green?

61

Answer Key

Numbers

The child picks 7 pretty flowers.
Can you color the 7 flowers red?

62

Numbers

The child kicks 8 balls.
Can you color the 8 balls black?

63

Numbers

9 birds are flying from the trees.
Can you color the 9 birds brown?

64

10 little rubber ducks float out at sea.
Can you color the 10 ducks yellow?

65

Counting

Can you count to 3?

1 2 3

Read the number.
Color that number of objects.

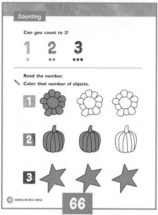

66

Can you trace the numbers?

1 2 3

Count the number of objects in each row.
Write the number on the line.

67

Counting

Can you count to 5?

1 2 3 4 5

Color 5 balls.

68

Can you trace the numbers?

1 2 3 4 5

Draw a line from the number to the correct
number of animals.

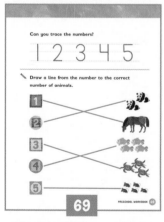

69

Counting

Help The Very Hungry Caterpillar turn into a butterfly.
Trace a path through the numbers from 1 to 10.

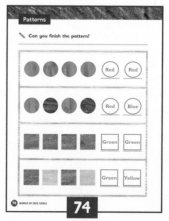

70

Connect the dots from 1 to 10.
What animal home did you make?

71

Counting

Count the number of objects in each row.
Write the number on the line.

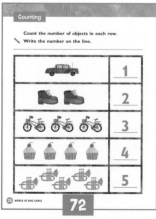

72

73

Patterns

Can you finish the pattern?

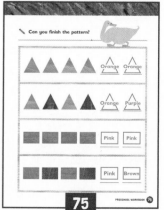

74

Can you finish the pattern?

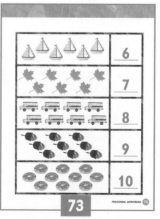

75

Page 76
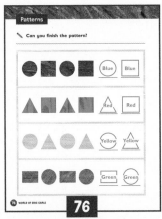
Patterns
Can you finish the pattern?
Blue Blue
Red Red
Yellow Yellow
Green Green
76 WORLD OF ERIC CARLE

Page 77
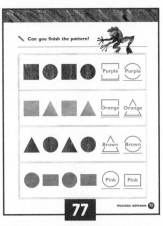
Can you finish the pattern?
Purple Purple
Orange Orange
Brown Brown
Pink Pink
77 PRESCHOOL WORKBOOK

Page 78
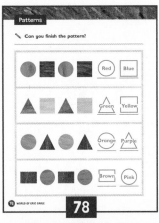
Patterns
Can you finish the pattern?
Red Blue
Green Yellow
Orange Purple
Brown Pink
78 WORLD OF ERIC CARLE

Page 79
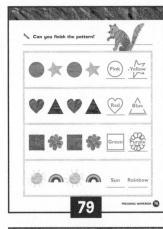
Can you finish the pattern?
Pink Yellow
Red Blue
Green Purple
Sun Rainbow
79 PRESCHOOL WORKBOOK

Page 80
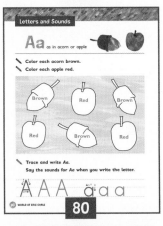
Letters and Sounds
Aa as in acorn or apple
Color each acorn brown.
Color each apple red.
Brown Red Brown
Red Brown Red
Trace and write Aa.
Say the sounds for Aa when you write the letter.
A A A a a a
80 WORLD OF ERIC CARLE

Page 81

Letters and Sounds
Bb as in bear
Color each picture that begins with Bb.
Trace and write Bb.
Say the sound for Bb when you write the letter.
B B B b b b
81 PRESCHOOL WORKBOOK

Page 82

Letters and Sounds
Cc as in cow
Can you help The Very Hungry Caterpillar find the cupcake?
Trace the path of cupcakes through the maze.
Trace and write Cc.
Say the sound for Cc when you write the letter.
C C C c c c
82 WORLD OF ERIC CARLE

Page 83

Letters and Sounds
Dd as in dinosaur
Circle each picture that begins with Dd.
Trace and write Dd.
Say the sound for Dd when you write the letter.
D D D d d d
83 PRESCHOOL WORKBOOK

Page 84

Letters and Sounds
Ee as in eagle or elephant
Color each eagle brown.
Color each elephant gray.
Gray Brown
Brown Gray
Trace and write Ee.
Say the sounds for Ee when you write the letter.
E E E e e e
84 WORLD OF ERIC CARLE

Page 85

Letters and Sounds
Ff as in fish
Color each picture that begins with Ff.
Trace and write Ff.
Say the sound for Ff when you write the letter.
F F F f f f
85 PRESCHOOL WORKBOOK

Page 86

Letters and Sounds
Gg as in grapes
Can you help the goat find the grass?
Trace the path of goats through the maze.
Trace and write Gg.
Say the sound for Gg when you write the letter.
G G G g g g
86 WORLD OF ERIC CARLE

Page 87

Letters and Sounds
Hh as in horse
Color each picture that begins with Hh.
Trace and write Hh.
Say the sound for Hh when you write the letter.
H H H h h h
87 PRESCHOOL WORKBOOK

Page 88
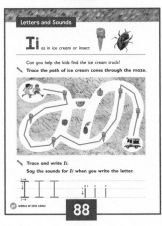
Letters and Sounds
Ii as in ice cream or insect
Can you help the kids find the ice cream truck!
Trace the path of ice cream cones through the maze.
Trace and write Ii.
Say the sounds for Ii when you write the letter.
I I I i i i
88 WORLD OF ERIC CARLE

Page 89

Letters and Sounds
Jj as in jam
Color each jar purple.
Color each jacket red.
Red Purple
Purple Red Red
Trace and write Jj.
Say the sound for Jj when you write the letter.
J J J j j j
89 PRESCHOOL WORKBOOK

Page 90

Letters and Sounds
Kk as in key
Circle each picture that begins with Kk.
Trace and write Kk.
Say the sound for Kk when you write the letter.
K K K k k k
90 WORLD OF ERIC CARLE

PRESCHOOL WORKBOOK 111

Answer Key

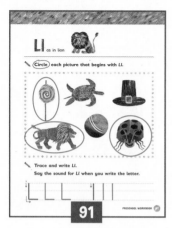

Ll as in lion

◟ Circle each picture that begins with *Ll*.

◟ Trace and write *Ll*.
Say the sound for *Ll* when you write the letter.

L L L l l l

91

Letters and Sounds

Mm as in mouse

◟ Circle each picture that begins with *Mm*.

◟ Trace and write *Mm*.
Say the sound for *Mm* when you write the letter.

M M M m m m

92

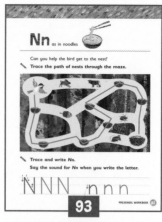

Nn as in noodles

◟ Can you help the bird get to the nest?
◟ Trace the path of nests through the maze.

◟ Trace and write *Nn*.
Say the sound for *Nn* when you write the letter.

N N N n n n

93

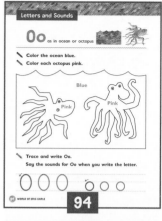

Letters and Sounds

Oo as in ocean or octopus

◟ Color the ocean blue.
◟ Color each octopus pink.

Blue
Pink   Pink

◟ Trace and write *Oo*.
Say the sounds for *Oo* when you write the letter.

O O O o o o

94

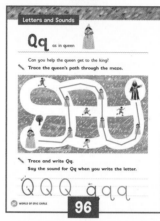

Pp as in pineapple

◟ Color each picture that begins with *Pp*.

◟ Trace and write *Pp*.
Say the sound for *Pp* when you write the letter.

P P P p p p

95

Letters and Sounds

Qq as in queen

◟ Can you help the queen get to the king?
◟ Trace the queen's path through the maze.

◟ Trace and write *Qq*.
Say the sound for *Qq* when you write the letter.

Q Q Q q q q

96

Rr as in rainbow

◟ Circle each picture that begins with *Rr*.

◟ Trace and write *Rr*.
Say the sound for *Rr* when you write the letter.

R R R r r r

97

Letters and Sounds

Ss as in spider

◟ Color each picture that begins with *Ss*.

◟ Trace and write *Ss*.
Say the sound for *Ss* when you write the letter.

S S S s s s

98

Tt as in trumpet

◟ Circle each picture that begins with *Tt*.

◟ Trace and write *Tt*.
Say the sound for *Tt* when you write the letter.

T T T t t t

99

Letters and Sounds

Uu as in unicorn or umbrella

◟ Color each unicorn pink.
◟ Color each umbrella purple.

Purple   Purple
Pink
Pink

◟ Trace and write *Uu*.
Say the sounds for *Uu* when you write the letter.

U U U u u u

100

Vv as in violin

◟ Can you put the flowers in the vase?
◟ Trace the path of flowers through the maze.

◟ Trace and write *Vv*.
Say the sound for *Vv* when you write the letter.

V V V v v v

101

Letters and Sounds

Ww as in walrus

◟ Circle each picture that begins with *Ww*.

◟ Trace and write *Ww*.
Say the sound for *Ww* when you write the letter.

W W W w w w

102

Xx as in X-ray

◟ Can you help the child find the fox?
◟ Trace the path of foxes through the maze.

◟ Trace and write *Xx*.
Say the sound for *Xx* when you write the letter.

X X X x x x

103

Letters and Sounds

Yy as in yellow yo-yo

◟ Circle each object that is yellow, like the yellow yo-yo.

◟ Trace and write *Yy*.
Say the sound for *Yy* when you write the letter.

Y Y Y y y y

104

Zz as in zebra

◟ Can you help the zebra find the zoo!
◟ Trace the path of zebras through the maze.

◟ Trace and write *Zz*.
Say the sound for *Zz* when you write the letter.

Z Z Z z z z

105